Children and the AIDS Virus

A BOOK FOR CHILDREN, PARENTS, & TEACHERS

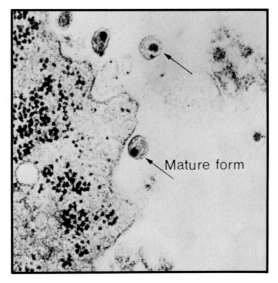

A photograph of the AIDS virus as
seen through an electron microscope.

Clarion Books
New York

For Jonathan and Celeste, and for all the other children
who have AIDS

Publisher's Note: The Author is donating a portion of her
royalty earnings to Children's Immunology Research Fund,
Inc., and to Camp Sunburst, a summer camp for children
with HIV, ARC, or AIDS.

Photo credits: All photographs are by the author except AIDS
virus on title page, courtesy of The Center for Disease Control,
Atlanta, Georgia; hair cell on page 6, courtesy of Mount Sinai
Medical Center, New York; and mosquito on page 17, courtesy of
American Museum of Natural History, Neg. #323290.

Clarion Books
a Houghton Mifflin Company imprint
52 Vanderbilt Avenue, New York, NY 10017
Text and photographs copyright © 1989 by Rosmarie Hausherr

Library of Congress Cataloging-in-Publication Data
Hausherr, Rosmarie.
   Children and the AIDS virus: a book for children, parents, and
teachers/Rosmarie Hausherr.
      p.   cm.
   Bibliography: p.
   Includes index.
   Summary: Explains in simple terms the body's immune system, how it
is attacked by the AIDS virus, and what can be done to prevent the
disease. The text is divided into a main text for the young reader
and an informational subtext for adults.
   ISBN 0-89919-834-1
   PA ISBN 0-395-51167-4
   1. AIDS (Disease) in children—Juvenile literature.   2. AIDS
(Disease)—Juvenile literature.   [1. AIDS (Disease)]   I. Title.
RJ387.A25H38   1989
618.92'9792—dc19   88-39196
                                    CIP
                                    AC
H   10 9 8 7 6 5 4 3 2 1

Acknowledgments

I deeply appreciate the generous support I received from more than one hundred people while I was researching, writing, and photographing this book. My thanks to everyone who participated in the photographs, especially Sheila and Jonathan, Toy and Celeste; and all the friends, in particular William J. Lederer and the Marunas family, who supplied encouragement, information, and contacts. I am grateful to the following institutions for professional assistance: New York University Medical Center, New York; Mount Sinai Medical Center, New York; Albert Einstein College of Medicine, Bronx, New York; Women and AIDS Resource Network, New York; and Third Street Music School, New York.

The following people gave me valuable advice on the manuscript: Carol Martinez Weber, M.D., Department of Community Medicine, St. Vincent's Hospital and Medical Center, New York; Steven Arkins, M.D., Pediatric Hematology, Mount Sinai Medical Center, New York; Lloyd Thomas, M.D., Lyndonville, VT; Geri Brooks, Ph.D., Director of the Children with HIV/AIDS Program, Tiburon, CA; Mariel Hess, R.N., F.N.P., Danville, VT; Marion Greenwood, Educational Director, Corlears School, New York; Marilyn Richards, Epidemiological Investigator, Burlington, VT; Anita Septimus, Pediatric AIDS Program Social Worker Coordinator, Albert Einstein Hospital, Bronx, NY; Ginny Moore Kruse, Director, Cooperative Children's Book Center, University of Wisconsin, Madison, WI; Kathleen Horning, Special Collections Coordinator, Cooperative Children's Book Center, University of Wisconsin, Madison, WI; Marge Sutinen, Acting Director, AIDS Support Network, Madison, WI; and Christine Jenkins, school librarian, Ann Arbor, MI.

I am grateful to my editor, Ann Troy, for guiding me with enthusiasm and patience. My thanks to Carol Goldenberg and Anthony Kramer for their creative design. Special thanks to Arye Rubinstein, M.D., Department of Pediatrics and Immunology at Albert Einstein College of Medicine in New York, who commented on the book in its final form.

A Note to Parents and Teachers

When you are using this book with a young child, you may want to read aloud just the main text, which is printed in large type. The text in smaller type is meant to give older children and adults more detailed information about subjects discussed in the main text.

Look in the mirror. What do you see?
A good-looking kid?
Yes, that's you!

   Look closer. Your body has different parts—a head, arms, and legs. These parts have smaller parts. Your arms have hands, your hands have fingers, and the fingers have nails.

Look even closer. Can you see fine hairs on the back of your hand? These hairs are made up of even smaller parts called *cells*. A cell is so tiny that you cannot see it without a microscope.

Your whole body is made up of billions of living cells. Your skin, your nails, your muscles, bones, blood, even your heart—every single part of you—are cells.

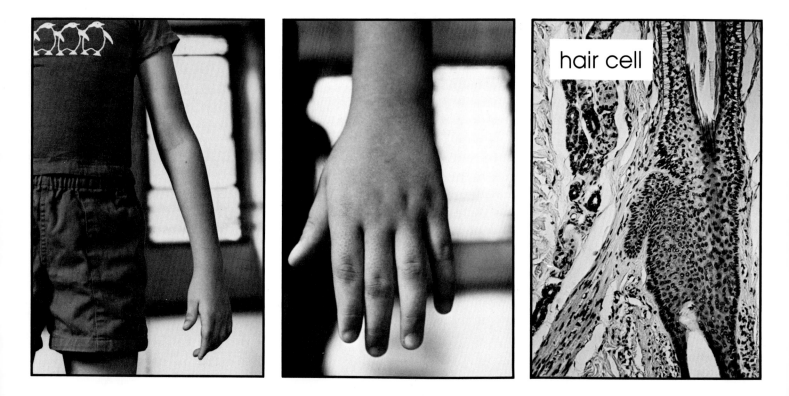

hair cell

All around you, outside of your body, live tiny things called *microorganisms*. They are invisible like cells. Microorganisms, such as bacteria, viruses, parasites, and fungi, are often harmless. But some of them can make you ill if they invade your body.

Inside your body, millions of special cells are ready to fight off invaders. Your fighter cells protect you. They are your body's natural defense system.

Let's find out about your *fighter cells* and one of their enemies, *viruses*.

Do you know what happened the last time you had a cold?

A cold virus sneaked inside your nose or throat and quickly made more viruses. But your fighter cells discovered the invaders and attacked them. All this activity upset your body and made you sick.

Luckily, your body's defense system was strong. Your fighter cells killed the viruses, and you felt better.

All viruses are invisible to the human eye. To see them, scientists use an *electron microscope*. This special instrument magnifies viruses thousands of times their original size.

The body has three types of fighter cells: *T cells, B cells,* and *phagocytes.* All of them together make up the natural immune defense system. B cells are known as "white blood cells."

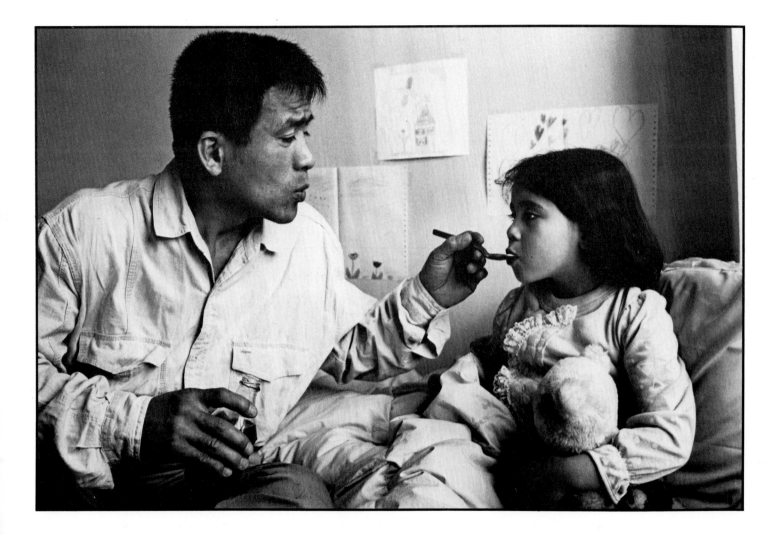

Not only children get the cold virus. Adults, like your mom and dad, catch it, too.

Where does the virus come from?

When a person with a cold sneezes, tiny droplets containing the cold virus fly through the air and land on anyone who is nearby. The virus can enter the body through the mouth, nose, or eyes. Because the virus is invisible, you never know when you get it.

Having a cold is no fun. But medicine, loving care, and rest can make you feel better.

Under the microscope, each type of virus looks unique. One kind will have a smooth surface. Another will have spikes. Each type of virus causes a different disease.

No medicine kills the cold virus. But cough syrup, nose spray, or hot liquids can help when the body hurts.

Other viruses can make you more ill than the cold virus does. Measles, mumps, rubella, chicken pox, and polio viruses also try to invade your body.

Before you were two years old, a doctor or nurse gave you a special vaccination shot. The vaccine made your fighter cells so strong they could chase away the measles, mumps, or rubella virus. The vaccine made you immune. That means the virus could not make you ill.

A vaccine is a medical preparation, usually injected into the arm. The polio vaccine is swallowed. There is no vaccine against chicken pox yet. Some vaccines protect from diseases caused by bacteria.

The body is immune when the fighter cells can easily identify and fight off a certain virus, or other harmful organism, that tries to infect it.

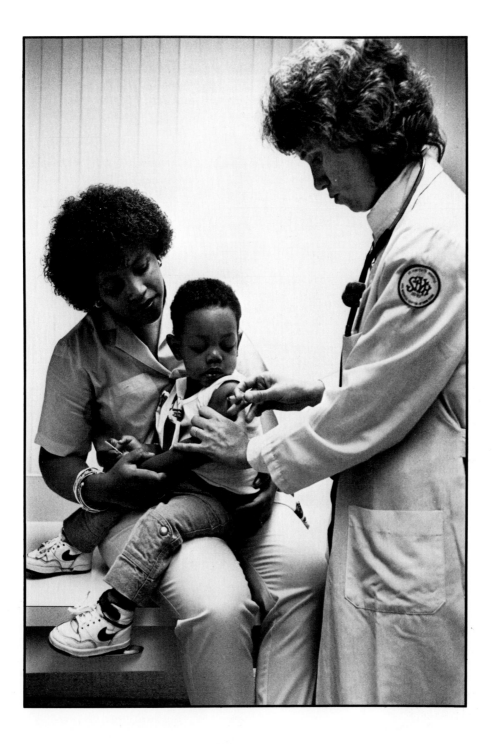

A few years ago, doctors discovered a new virus: the HIV, or AIDS virus, which can cause AIDS. What happens when a person has this virus?

Sometimes the AIDS virus stays in the cells without doing harm. The person remains healthy.

In other people, the AIDS virus multiplies and begins attacking fighter cells. That can make these people a little sick. They have ARC.

But, in some people, the AIDS virus kills many fighter cells. Without fighter cells, the body has no protection against harmful microorganisms. Bacteria, fungi, and common viruses can make these people ill with dangerous diseases. These people have AIDS.

Doctors identified the AIDS virus in 1984. They call it the HIV – human immunodeficiency virus. It causes the loss of immunity in the human body. The word *AIDS* is put together from four other words: A = acquired, I = immune, D = deficiency, S = syndrome.

ARC means AIDS-related complex. People with ARC have a number of medical problems, but they are not seriously ill. Many, but not all, people who have ARC will later develop AIDS.

Doctors are studying the AIDS virus to learn why it attacks the immune system in some infected people and not in others.

It is important to learn about the AIDS virus. You will be glad to know that children almost never get this virus.

You do not catch it from a person's sneeze the way you catch the cold virus. No one gets AIDS from being around people or from touching them. You can't pick up the AIDS virus from things you share with others.

Outside the human body, the AIDS virus dies quickly. For its survival, it needs a host cell in the human body. After penetrating a T cell in the immune system, the virus multiplies until the host cell bursts and dies.

Each spewed-out virus then repeats the process. Each type of virus chooses its own specific kind of host cell.

pets

doorknobs

toys

toilets

money

a kiss

insects

sharing food

touching

Usually, the AIDS virus cannot enter our body through the skin. It has to find other ways to get into the blood.

Let's find out how this can happen.

There are people who use illegal drugs. Some inject these dangerous drugs into the body with a needle. They share the needle with other drug users. If one of the drug users has AIDS, the virus could be in the blood that is on the needle. The next person who uses that needle may inject the AIDS virus into his or her own body.

The HIV travels in the blood to different parts of the body.

Doctors can tell from a special blood test if a person is HIV-infected. Infected means that a virus, bacteria, or other parasite has invaded a person's body.

If HIV-infected blood comes in contact with skin that has sores, cuts, or lesions, the virus could enter the body through these openings.

There is no risk of contracting a virus from injections given by health care professionals. Their needles and syringes are sterile and used only one time.

There is another way the AIDS virus can get inside a person's body and into the blood – from body fluid.

When people have sex, body fluid can go from one person to the other. If one of the two people has the AIDS virus, the tiny virus can slide with the body fluid inside the other person. From there, the AIDS virus finds its way into the blood.

Body fluid is "body water." We have different fluids in our body: tears, saliva (spit), and urine. Men have semen and women have vaginal fluids in their private parts.

The HIV has been found in semen and in vaginal fluids. But only small numbers of the virus have been detected in saliva and tears.

The AIDS virus is dangerous because an infected adult may look and feel healthy and not know the virus is in the body. If that person has sex, the sex partner may become infected, too.

To help protect themselves against receiving or spreading the HIV, many people practice *safer sex* . They use a condom. A condom, also called a *rubber*, is a thin piece of latex that encloses the penis. A condom prevents the exchange of body fluids.

As you get older, you may have questions about sex. Ask a parent, teacher, or another adult you trust for answers. Or you may want to read some of the wonderful and informative children's books on the subject of sex that are available at most school and public libraries.

Young children do not catch the AIDS virus as long as they do not inject illegal drugs and do not have sex.

But...haven't you heard about children who have AIDS?

Five-year-old Jonathan, who enjoys flying paper airplanes and playing Superman, has AIDS. When Jonathan was little, he became ill and needed a blood transfusion. This means blood from somebody else was put into his body. The AIDS virus was in that blood, but the doctors didn't know it. When Jonathan became ill again, they found AIDS viruses in his body.

Today, Jonathan regularly gets products from healthy blood to boost his fighter cells. But now the hospital carefully tests the blood to make sure it is safe.

Hospitals keep donated blood in blood banks. Since March 1985, all blood in blood banks is checked for the HIV. Donating blood is always safe.

Some children and adults are born with blood that doesn't clot properly — a condition called *hemophilia*. When hemophiliacs are injured, they don't stop bleeding easily. They need a special clotting substance from donated blood. Before 1985, some hemophiliacs received HIV-contaminated blood.

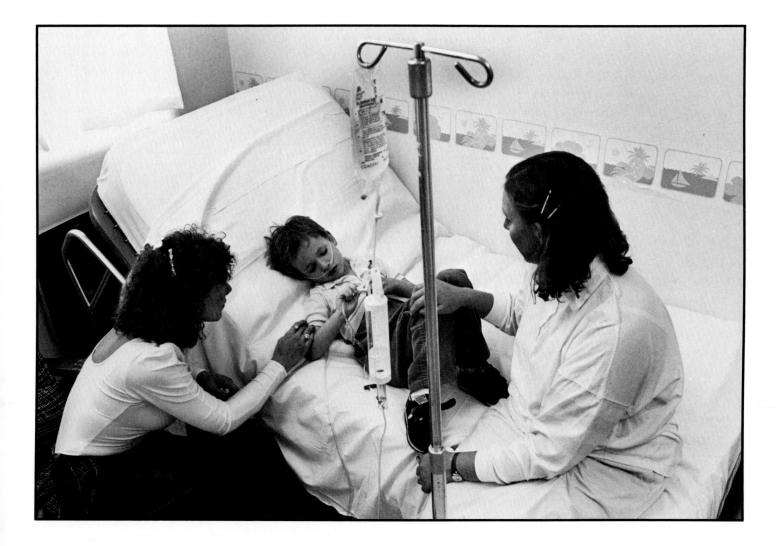

Jonathan is healthy enough to go to school. The AIDS virus has not killed too many of his fighter cells. He still has enough of them to defend his body.

Some parents in his community didn't want Jonathan to attend school. They were afraid their own children would catch the AIDS virus from him. But doctors told teachers and parents that it is safe to share the classroom with a child who has AIDS.

Doctors will tell you that you can play with a child who has AIDS. You can swim in the same pool, visit each other's house, watch a movie, share toys, and enjoy snacks together. You can even share funny secrets with a friend who has AIDS.

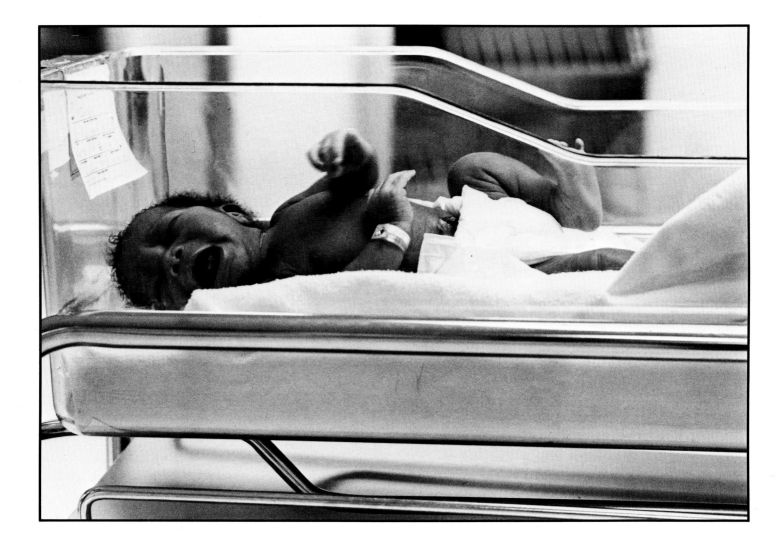

Some babies are born with the AIDS virus. They caught the virus from their mothers who have AIDS. Babies with AIDS are often sick, and many need hospital care. Some die when they are still little. But as doctors and nurses keep learning about the virus, they are able to help more children survive.

More HIV-infected babies have been born in the last few years because more mothers have AIDS.

The HIV has spread throughout the world, and many adults and children have suffered and died from AIDS.

Celeste's tenth birthday was a happy event for her family, doctor, nurses, and social workers. Ten years ago, Celeste was born with AIDS. She got the virus from her mother. Over the years, the AIDS virus killed many of Celeste's fighter cells. Her body was not protected, and invaders kept making her ill.

But doctors keep strengthening Celeste's fighter cells by giving her products from healthy blood. She is well enough to attend school, where she learns and plays like any other child.

Doctors and nurses are doing their best to make Jonathan and Celeste and other people with AIDS feel better when they are sick. But there is no medicine yet that kills the AIDS virus. Because there is no cure, adults and children with AIDS often die.

In hospitals and laboratories, doctors and scientists are working hard to find medicine that will heal all AIDS-infected people.

Intensive AIDS research is conducted in many countries. Scientists have made remarkable progress, but they still face unsolved problems.

AIDS medicines are being developed and tested. Today only a few are available to AIDS patients. A drug called AZT does not offer a cure, but it seems to slow down the destruction of the immune system caused by the HIV.

Years ago, people suffered and died from measles, mumps, polio, and other serious diseases caused by viruses. Then scientists found vaccines to protect everyone.

Today scientists are searching again. This time they are determined to find a vaccine that will make us immune to AIDS.

For now, understanding how the AIDS virus is spread can take away our fear of catching it. We can enjoy having a friend with AIDS because we know it is safe to play together, to hug each other, and to share funny secrets.

More about Jonathan and his mother, Sheila

Jonathan lives with his mother and his older brothers in a suburb of Denver, Colorado. Like any five-year-old child, he plays, rides his bike, and sometimes gets into mischief. Jonathan has breathing difficulties caused by the AIDS virus. To help him get enough oxygen, he wears a long, thin tube that connects him to an oxygen tank in the house.

Jonathan needed a blood transfusion shortly after his premature birth. But the donated blood he received was contaminated with the AIDS virus. As a result, he became ill with dangerous infectious diseases. However, doctors did not suspect the HIV to be the cause. When Jonathan was diagnosed as having AIDS, it came as a terrible shock to his mother, Sheila.

The members of Jonathan's family felt like outcasts because frightened neighbors shunned them. Life became difficult. At first, Sheila was bitter and angry, especially at gay (homosexual) men, the largest population group diagnosed with AIDS. Perhaps a gay person who did not know he was HIV-infected donated the blood that Jonathan received. Nevertheless, it was the gay community, through an organization called PFLAG – Parents and Friends of Lesbians and Gays – who first offered support to Sheila and her family. Jonathan got a "buddy," a special friend, from the Colorado AIDS Project. His buddy is a young man who visits him at home or takes him to the zoo, a museum, or another interesting place.

As Jonathan's neighbors learned more about his disease, they became supportive. After his mother won an eight-month battle with the school district, Jonathan started attending school with other children. He carries a portable oxygen tank to the classroom.

At the hospital, Jonathan receives biweekly gamma globulin, antibodies from human blood serum. The antibodies protect Jonathan from common infections. Sheila keeps herself informed of the latest medical developments. She knows Jonathan could die soon, but she hopes he will live a long life.

With Sheila's permission, Jonathan was photographed without wearing the oxygen line. This was safe to do. We wanted to avoid the impression that all children with AIDS need oxygen. Jonathan's inner lung lining is inflamed. This is a secondary consequence of the AIDS virus and, hopefully, only a temporary condition.

More about Celeste and her grandmother, Toy

Celeste, a petite ten-year-old girl, is the oldest known survivor born with AIDS.

She lives with her grandmother, Toy, in the South Bronx, in New York. Celeste's two older sisters, two cousins, and an aunt live with them as well. The story of her family is not uncommon in large urban ghettos. Her mother and father, both intravenous drug users, contracted AIDS. As a result, Celeste and her younger brother, Eddie, were born HIV-infected.

When Celeste's mother and father died of AIDS, Toy managed to keep the rest of the family together. She cared for Celeste and Eddie, who were often ill with infectious diseases caused by the AIDS virus. The children needed numerous treatments at the Albert Einstein Hospital in the Bronx. Celeste survived several operations.

Toy and her family – like Sheila in Denver – were ostracized by frightened friends and neighbors who had heard about the family's AIDS problems. Celeste and Eddie, who were not told that they had AIDS, could not understand why no other children would play with them. At that time, there were no AIDS-outreach programs in the South Bronx. Continuous support from the doctors, nurses, and social workers from the pediatric AIDS department at the Albert Einstein Hospital helped Toy and her grand-children through difficult times. Then, at age five, Eddie died.

Today Celeste is able to go to school thanks to the regular intravenous gamma-globulin treatments she receives at the hospital. Her social worker says Celeste does well in school and receives good grades despite her numerous health-related absences, caused by the AIDS virus.

An essay on the subject of AIDS and children in a national magazine featured Celeste on the cover. This brought attention and some support to the family. Recently, Celeste was invited to spend a vacation at Camp Sunburst, a special summer camp in California for HIV-infected children and children who have ARC or AIDS.

Health care precautions:

It has been established that the AIDS virus can be transmitted through contact with HIV-contaminated blood. In our day-by-day interaction with adults and children, we do not know who is HIV-infected. For this reason, health care professionals recommend the following precautions:

• Children or adults should not share toothbrushes. HIV-infected blood could be transmitted from bleeding gums.

• If a child or adult bleeds (from a nosebleed or cut, for example), avoid direct contact with the blood. This also applies to body fluids, such as urine. Use rubber gloves and clean soiled surfaces with a household disinfectant, such as bleach, diluted one part to ten parts water.

• If an uninfected child bites a child with AIDS, the risk of getting the HIV would exist only if the bite broke the skin and caused bleeding. So far, there are no known cases of AIDS having been transmitted by an infected child biting an uninfected child. Children should be taught not to bite others.

• Children sometimes seal friendships by becoming "blood brothers" or "blood sisters." They each prick a finger and touch each other's blood, declaring lifelong friendship. Since the AIDS virus is transmitted by blood, parents should discourage their children from performing this ritual.

These brochures provide helpful answers to questions about caring for children with AIDS. The pamphlets were in print in 1988, although they may not be available by the time you read this book. Please get in touch with the organizations listed below for more information.

AIDS: 100 Questions and Answers
New York State Health Department
Box 2000
Albany, NY 12220

Available in English and Spanish

Recommended Precautions for Caretakers of Children with AIDS
Pediatric AIDS Hotline
Albert Einstein College of Medicine
Room F-401
1300 Morris Park Avenue
Bronx, NY 10461

Available in English and Spanish

Children with AIDS:
Guidelines for Parents and Caregivers
The AIDS Task Force of Central New York
P.O. Box 1911
Syracuse, NY 13201
or
Hemophilia Council of California
2206 K Street
Suite 4
Sacramento, CA 95816

What we can do about AIDS

According to medical experts, the number of people infected with and dying of AIDS is increasing in this country and throughout the world. Despite intense medical research, an AIDS cure or vaccine is not likely to be available in the near future. AIDS will be with us for years to come. Are we in a hopeless situation? No, because there is much that each of us can do:

• We can become informed about AIDS from reliable, accurate sources and avoid getting and spreading the virus.

• We can educate our children about sex and AIDS with a positive attitude.

• We can talk frankly with our children about drugs and alcohol. If we find this difficult, we can get assistance from a teacher, social worker, or drug counselor.

• If a friend or neighbor is diagnosed as having AIDS, we can be the same helpful friend we have always been. At work, we can treat a colleague who has AIDS with dignity.
We can let our children know that it is all right to be friends with a child or adult who has AIDS.

• In school board or town meetings, we can support efforts to allow children with AIDS to go to schools and to use recreational facilities. We can say yes to a proposed AIDS hospice or child care home in our neighborhood.

• We can participate in fund-raising for the AIDS cause.

If you are ready for a more involved commitment:

• You can join a local AIDS support group and become a volunteer, or "buddy," a friend and supporter to a child or an adult who has AIDS.

• You can become a foster or adoptive parent to a child with AIDS. Many orphaned or abandoned HIV-infected children are in need of loving care and a good home.

Resources

National AIDS Network
1012 14th Street NW
Suite 601
Washington, DC 20005
202-293-2437
The National AIDS Network (NAN) publishes a directory with a complete listing of over 450 community, state, national, and international AIDS education and service organizations. NAN also distributes AIDS-related periodicals, books, videos, and newsletters, and sponsors workshops and conferences.

U.S. Public Health Service:
AIDS Hotline 1-800-342-AIDS
1-800-342-2437

AIDS Action Council
Washington, DC
202-293-2886

Children with HIV-AIDS Program
Tiburon, CA
415-435-5022

The Foundation for Children with AIDS
Brighton, MA
617-783-7300

National AIDS Information Clearing House
Rockville, MD
800-458-5231

National Association of People with AIDS
Suite 415
Washington, DC
202-429-2856

The National Hemophilia Foundation
National Resource and Consultation Center
   for AIDS and HIV Information (New York)
212-219-8180

National Minority AIDS Council
Washington, DC
202-544-1076

Northern Lights Alternatives
New York, NY
212-337-8747

Albert Einstein College of Medicine
Bronx, NY
Pediatric and Pregnancy
AIDS Hotline: 212-430-3333

Women and AIDS Resource Network
New York, NY
718-596-6007

Camp Sunburst is a summer camp for children who have HIV, ARC, or AIDS and their families. For more information about Camp Sunburst and its activities, contact Geri Brooks, Ph.D., Executive Director, Camp Sunburst, 148 Wilson Hall Road, Petaluma, CA 94952; 707-763-4782.

SIECUS
Sex Information and Education Council of the U.S.
New York University
32 Washington Place
New York, NY 10003
212-673-3850

Bibliography

The Albert Einstein College of Medicine/ Montefiore Medical Center. *Recommended Precautions for Caretakers of Children with AIDS.* New York, 1988.

The American College Health Association. *Making Sex Safer.* Rockville, Md., 1987.

American Council of Life Insurance and Health Insurance Association of America. *Teens & AIDS: Playing It Safe.* 1987.

Barrett, Douglas J. "The Clinician's Guide to Pediatric AIDS." *Contemporary Pediatrics* 5 (January 1988): 24–47.

Friedland, Gerald H., and Robert S. Klein. "Transmission of the Human Immuno-deficiency Virus." *The New England Journal of Medicine* 317, no. 18 (October 29, 1987): 1125–1135.

Jaret, Peter. "Our Immune System: The Wars Within." *National Geographic,* June 1986, 702–734.

Joseph, Stephen C. "Women with AIDS: The New York City Experience." Lecture presented at symposium, "Women and AIDS," sponsored by College of Physicians and Surgeons of Columbia University, New York, September 1987.

Knight, David C. *Your Body's Defenses.* New York: McGraw-Hill Book Co., 1975.

Kolata, Gina. "AIDS Virus Found to Hide in Cells, Eluding Detection by Normal Tests." *New York Times,* June 5, 1988, 1, 28.

_____. "Children and AIDS: Drug Tests Raise Hope and Ethical Concerns." *New York Times*, May 24, 1988, C3.

_____. "The Evolving Biology of AIDS: Scavenger Cell Looms Large." *New York Times,* June 7, 1988, C1, C8.

Krim, Mathilde. "Ethical Issues in the AIDS Epidemic." Lecture presented at symposium, "Women and AIDS," sponsored by College of Physicians and Surgeons of Columbia University, New York, September 1987.

Levine, Stephen B. *Let's Talk about Sex.* New York: The National Hemophilia Foundation, 1988.

Moglia, Ronald, and Ann Welbourne-Moglia. *How to Talk to Your Children about AIDS.* New York: New York University and SIECUS, 1986.

Monmaney, Terence. "Kids with AIDS." *Newsweek,* September 7, 1987, 36–46.

The National Hemophilia Foundation. *What You Should Know about Hemophilia.* New York, 1988.

The New York City Department of Health. "Pediatric AIDS." *City Health Information* 5, no. 2 (February 19–March 12, 1986).

New York State Department of Health. *AIDS: 100 Questions and Answers.* Albany, 1987.

New York State Department of Health. *A Physician's Guide to HIV Counseling and Testing.* Albany, 1987.

Pitt, Jane. "Children of Women with AIDS." Lecture presented at symposium, "Women and AIDS," sponsored by College of Physicians and Surgeons of Columbia University, New York, September 1987.

Ralston, Alissa. *What Do Our Children Need to Know about AIDS? Guidelines for Parents.* Novato, Calif.: Beneficial Publishing, 1988.

Scott, Gwendolyn B., Margaret A. Fischl, and Nancy Klimas, et al. "Mothers of Infants with the Acquired Immunodeficiency Syndrome." *The Journal of the American Medical Association* 255, no. 3 (January 18, 1985): 363–366.

Selwyn, Peter A. "AIDS: What Is Now Known: II. Epidemiology." *Hospital Practice,* June 15, 1986, 127–164.

Tanne, Janice Hopkins. "Fighting AIDS." *New York,* January 12, 1987, 23–31.

U.S. Department of Health and Human Services. *Facts about AIDS,* 1987.

——————. *Surgeon General's Report on Acquired Immune Deficiency Syndrome.*

——————. *Understanding AIDS.* Rockville, Md., 1988.

U.S. Department of Health and Human Services, Centers for Disease Control. "Guidelines for Effective School Health Education to Prevent the Spread of AIDS." *Morbidity and Mortality Weekly Report* 37, no. S–2 (January 29, 1988): 1–14.

Wallis, Claudia. "Viruses: AIDS Research Spurs New Interest in Some Ancient Enemies." *Time,* November 3, 1986, 66–74.

Worth, Dooley, and Ruth Rodriguez. "Latina Women and AIDS." *SIECUS Report,* January–February 1987, 5–6.

The poster "I HAVE AIDS—Please Hug Me—I Can't Make You Sick," by artist Jack Keeler, is available for a $5.00 donation for each copy from:

Children with HIV/AIDS Program
The Center for Attitudinal Healing
19 Main Street
Tiburon, CA 94920

Index

Page numbers in *italics* refer to illustrations.